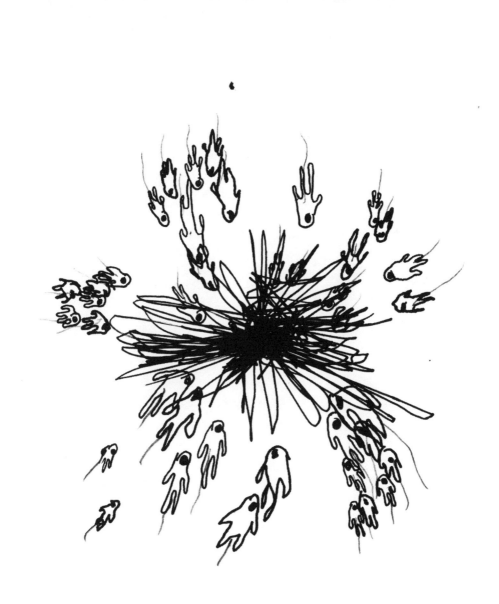

THE SUNFLOWER CAST A SPELL
TO SAVE US FROM THE VOID

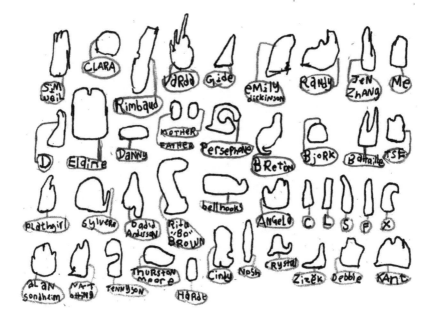

The Sunflower Cast a Spell to Save Us from the Void

WORDS BY

Jackie Wang

ILLUSTRATIONS BY

Kalan Sherrard

Nightboat Books

NEW YORK

ISBN: 978-1-64362-036-7

Cover Photo: Theresa Wang

Film stills credits:
The Mirror, 1975, Andrei Tarkovsky, Kino Lorber
The Sacrifice, 1986, Andrei Tarkovsky, Kino Lorber

Design and typesetting by Kit Schluter
Text set in Helvetica and EB Garamond

Cataloging-in-publication data
is available from the Library of Congress

Nightboat Books
New York
www.nightboat.org

CONTENTS

For my family

"Is woman not always a you and never quite an I?"

VIRGINIA BURRUS, *The Sex Lives of Saints:
An Erotics of Ancient Hagiography*

TARKOVSKY'S CHIGNONS
TARKOVSKY'S CHIGNONS
TARKOVSKY'S CHIGNONS

(I dreamed I turned them in as my poems)

As flowers turn toward the sun, by dint of a secret heliotropism the past strives to turn toward that sun which is rising in the sky of history.

WALTER BENJAMIN

LIFE IS A PLACE WHERE IT'S FORBIDDEN TO LIVE

All I remember is the coppiced terrain I crossed to find a house to rest in. Who is the woman lurking in the woods? A fellow traveler. I'm not used to seeing others. She is lost and I am lost but the difference is she is a novice at being lost, whereas I have always been without country. Without planet. When we happen upon a cabin I ask the housie for shelter on her behalf. I'm aware that we come off as oogles but want to prove we are different by washing dishes. To concretize my gratitude.

In the morning, before the others awake, I set off for the holy site in a horse-drawn carriage. The carriage has a detachable sleeping chamber designed so that a princely man can carry me supine whenever the horse gets tired.

At sunset my pilgrimage is complete. The Asian market is a glass palace overlooking an airport. From outside the Palace of Snacks the products shine like organs inside a hard, translucent skin. As I take the palace escalator heavenward my eyes are fixed on an airplane parked on the runway.

It is waiting for me.

DEATH AS A SURVIVAL TECHNIQUE

The world is warming, and we humans are to blame. In the future the world will only hold one person, therefore everyone else must die. It is for this reason that I find myself in a Hunger Games caused by global warming. Everyone knows there can only be one survivor. The people are febrile with murderous rage. Though I do not intend to kill anyone I still must persuade everyone not to kill me. I have to get them to empathize with me. But I don't plead. Sometimes I hide by lying prone atop a pole pretending to be dead. By making myself visible I remove the anxiety of being found. My fake death becomes an orchestration that involves as many people as Tupac's pseudo-death.

In the distance I hear Maxine eulogize me. He knows I'm not dead but to stop people from killing me he must convince them I have died. Feigning death makes me privy to how I will be remembered. I think, *How sad that people are not alive to experience their funerals because it's the most love they'll ever get.* Maxine memorializes people in a way that only a queer who has lived through the AIDS crisis can.

Ah, but I'm alive!

The threat of death calms me.

On the shore there is a crumbling beach house culled from the iconography of *Eternal Sunshine of the Spotless Mind.*

Everything is crumbling as we wait for intermittent waves to hit.

Where, in this house, will I find air to breathe?

The walls won't hold. The safety I feel in this structure is false.

I am crouched in a corner waiting to die

Until Elijah comes and asks me to participate in a fashion show to "lighten the apocalyptic mood."

Elijah takes me to a warehouse, dresses me in skimpy clothes and pushes me on stage.

Ashamed of my body, I try to cover myself with my hands and arms.

From the audience he yells, "Show more belly!"

And then to celebrate my performance he takes me into an empty crumbling house to play me a song on the piano while the house fills with water.

Imminent apocalyptic obliteration has brought out everyone's repressed desires. All over the shore people are having BDSM sex in the ruins.

Where did all these leather belts come from, I think.

I see my friend all tied up, blissed-out, her eyes rolling back in her head.

It is a way to prepare for death.

The sadists believe they will be the ones who will survive.

The masochists embrace their powerlessness in the situation.

Freakish weather makes us all non-sovereign.

In this sense the sadists will be punished for their hubris: their belief that through sheer muscular will they can beat Mother Nature. The story becomes an epic showdown between sadists and masochists.

But I know that the situation calls for total passivity.

Maybe that doesn't make sense?

Maybe it's a pact with the gods.

The secret is to not try.

In giving yourself over to the inevitability of death, nothing can hurt you.

Nature no longer wants to kill you.

You have put yourself at the center of the battle of cosmic forces and lowered your sword.

Because you were willing to die, you will be spared.

But . . .

But.

I am sad that all my friends will die even if this situation has turned them against me.

Why must only one survive this environmental catastrophe?

To submit.

To take the passive road to heaven.

Survival of the fittest?

No.

Survival of the best at playing dead.

THE EVIL NOODLE

The little Asian girl, upon meeting her estranged sister, believes she will die if she eats a single noodle from the bowl sis gives her.

The mother tries to force the little girl to eat the noodles.

I want to intervene because—what if the girl is right? Do we really want to risk it?

Did I see the older sister slip an evil noodle into the bowl while nobody was looking?

I believe that the little girl knows intuitively when someone is trying to hurt her, though she is too young to explain how she knows what she knows.

She is about 3 years old, dark skin, long black hair.

She sits on the floor in a corner while her mother and older sister try to cajole her out of aloofness.

There was something false about the older sister's generosity. I saw it too.

I feel a kinship with the little girl because we can both sniff out evil.

But who am I?

Anonymous observer. Nobody sees me.

What is the noodle that radiates evil and why don't others see it?

COMPANION SPECIES

Once I went to see a performance by a guy from Paper Rad. While waiting for the set to begin I heard, for the first time, the song "Me and My Puppy"—a kind of anthem for lonely 11-year-olds looking for something to love. All over the world young girls were befriending creatures and trees and constructing fantasy worlds of reciprocated love.

While some lonely girls have puppies, I have a shapeshifting butterfly.

The monarch butterfly clings to me for years. It never leaves my body and I feel loved.

I don't want the butterfly to die. Ever.

The monarch crawls to the bottom of my foot and turns into a clouded sulphur: a common yellow butterfly.

Because it has shed its lepidopterous beauty in exchange for anonymity it no longer desires to come out to greet others.

It lives on the bottom of my foot.

With the butterfly using my body as its home I feel like somebody special . . . *chosen.*

People don't believe that the butterfly stays with me and their disbelief makes me crazy.

They think I'm making it up so I take my foot out of my shoe and there she is, little yellow wings.

INSTEAD OF THICKENING MY SKIN
I BUY A NEON BALACLAVA

I write a play that incites violence against me.

It is a twisted and tender portrait of the violence of girlhood and nascent lesbian desire.

While I am swimming in a pool, oblivious to the firestorm of controversy ignited by my play, a man comes to interview me. I am floating on a pink plastic raft in sunglasses.

I know this man and feel enmity behind his questions.

Though the man hates me he hates me with subtlety and equanimity. He is not like the hysterical hordes who plot to kill me by cutting my breaks and slipping arsenic into my porridge.

His hatred is a kind of respect.

In the interview he gets my influences right: *Innocence* by Lucile Hadžihalilović, the French lesbian film *Water Lilies* by Céline Sciamma, Violette Leduc, and the novels of Elfriede Jelinek.

This interviewer seems to know me.

While interviewing me he tells me about a dramaturge who ended her career after reading my play.

I am curious about the power of my play.

The indecent play's detractors are not primarily the morally righteous puritans who are driven mad by the mockery the play makes of their probity.

It's the insurrectionists who hate it most!

I ask the interviewer: Is it me they hate, or the play?

Many of the haters are my old friends.

The interviewer assures me it's the play.

My mother, who is on drugs, can't take the violence and chaos I have brought upon our household with my play.

I go to the library to escape public scrutiny.

At the library I secretly read the books the man referenced in his interview.

But the man has followed me to the library! Oh, this is embarrassing.

When I leave the library the alarm goes off because I have accidentally carried out a book.

Not knowing where to hide, I go to the mall to buy neon balaclavas.

Was I unconsciously trying to redeem myself in the eyes of the insurrectionists by buying the neon balaclavas?

The man has followed me here too. He's behind a rack of clothing, judging my sartorial selections.

As I feel myself seared by his stare I know that his scorn has turned to a kind of love.

It is possible I have mistaken his obsessive desire to possess me for love.

Repulsion, fascination, hatred, intrigue. This dance of ambivalent reactions, this tense intimacy ensnares me.

There is so much reaction that I only vaguely remember the content of the play.

Something about

Young girls at a French boarding school sneaking into each other's beds after the authoritarian headmistress has flicked off the lights.

What I enjoy about being hated the way the interviewer hates me is that he is, in a sense, my only witness.

What I don't enjoy about being seen the way the interviewer sees me is that there's nowhere to hide.

I pull a hot pink balaclava over my head to interrupt the event of recognition.

REFUGE

In the rain, in her head, an elegy for the not-quite-dead.

Some peonies placed beside her body, supine beneath the canopy of forgotten dreams.

She woke in such a state, such a state that she had to take shelter from the beloved's rain beneath a tree.

It rained so hard she didn't know where she was.

I don't like being left to myself like this.

THE FUTURE IS BETWEEN US

There is no corpus to clamber across to where you are, and thinking your absence just whets my appetite. I go to a Mexican diner alone to satisfy something else. But I don't recognize any of the dishes. The server stares at me; my strained cogitation must be visible on my face as I struggle to make sense of the menu. "I just . . . I just want beans and eggs!" I cry in a fit of frustration. As I'm ordering food my friend D calls to tell me I'm not a real person of color. When the food arrives I eat it in shame. Outside the diner the world is falling to pieces, but you would never know it in here. I don't want to leave! *Ever!* Because the catastrophe doesn't exist so long as I delay perceiving it. Can a book parry catastrophe? Let another temporality be my home! But death is everywhere in the book.

As soon as I take my book out of my backpack the server tells me to leave. "This isn't the place for that." In other words, it is time to face the judgment.

Outside, the air of apocalypse is all around as I walk beneath millions of satellites.

In the distance I see a familiar house. It is a life-size dollhouse where my old friend is raising her little brother. She tells me I can sleep on the couch.

Always, this nowhere-to-go.

I don't think about where I will go next.

While my friend tucks her little brother into a racecar-shaped bed I ask if I can use her computer to check my email.

"It's in the living room," she says without looking up.

But where is the computer?

The whole room is the computer—a retrofitted machine whose processors are concealed in the furniture.

The entire north-facing wall is taken up by an LCD screen that runs MS-DOS.

You are there when I log onto AOL Instant Messenger.

After all of these years, how do I remember the password?

Because the body of our book has been incinerated by the judgment I have to transmit consciousness diagonally, through the coiled spine of the immaterial nexus.

As a series of commands, you transmit beautiful poetry about the things you have seen.

But are you you? I am uneasy about the fact that I cannot verify it is you on the other end. You are writing to me with uncharacteristic effusiveness.

Revelation upon revelation scrolls on the giant LCD screen. About human sacrifice and religious experience, how everything felt boring after the riot.

It is too much! I want to pull away. Your scattershot epiphanies pierce me like bullets. I want a room just to sit in and contemplate what you are saying.

All I remember now: "hashtag of the future."

You were near the ocean when it happened.

And though you must speak around the event I somehow grasp it perfectly. Not through cerebration but through the real-time experience of the emotions it stirred in you.

Looking at the enormous LCD screen, I am confused about who wrote what! In the puddle of our psychic fusion, I could have written your part.

Then all of a sudden, I don't know what to say to you. You're in such a state. Such a state of ecstasy and I can't keep up. I want to follow you there.

But the mainframe between us is wilting, everything starts to break, the satellites are crashing into sad lights

And then it's just me alone with your poetry in the life-sized dollhouse, no way to respond.

The "there" (of "you") was both the ocean and the state (of divine perfection).

Before the technological catastrophe of separation I felt excited that there was at least one person with whom I could share the urgency of THINGS MUST BE DIFFERENT.

As in: after such an experience, things can never be the same.

Would having someone to travel with allow me to take it all the way?

WITHOUT TONGUE

The parts I tell you are often not the most important parts of the dream. I said we had shared a dream, that Masha, Nat and I stood around talking about the loveliness of your voice. When I spoke to you on the phone the morning before the dream you said the word "disavowed." Meaning collapsed into a quality of sound. What were you saying? I was telling you I had a shitty draft of a novel and though you trust my opinion (one should never trust a masochist's opinion of themselves), you have loved some of my "disavowed" writings. Because I noticed your voice, I had to dream it. When I reached for the phone to text you the morning of the dream I left out the part where you kissed me, devouringly, but without tongue. You were a snail on my lower lip, my mouth impossibly capacious. The kiss enervated us. After parting, we both (simultaneously but in separate locales) collapsed with exhaustion. When I woke from the second layer of dream into the first layer of dream I wanted to call you. On the phone you said, *I just napped*, and I said, *Me too*, and, *What did you dream?* I asked you that question once before, when you were on a bus to Philadelphia.

I dreamed...I dreamed I was in the Village of Religions.

I can't believe it.

We are inhabiting the same dream.

17

Depths Apocrypos...

propocalypticiis

Topographys

In the dream I mutter

Capitalism is not a bed of sunflowers

as I hobble around Wall Street

in broken high heels.

THE BAND OF INSURGENT ANGELS

All dream, all seam—this ribbon

The churned-up pink revolt when you are free to receive perfectly (unselfishly) the gift of decreation

Outlaw jouissance takes no substitute, returns to your door just to return, to stay, to touch or otherwise connect

Our fault-lined crypt finds the perfect parchment to catalog descent

To become destructed angels

And as destructed

open to all activities against the law and financial institutions

THE RESURRECTION OF ANGELA

The reading is held in the remodeled barn. I wait all night for my turn to read. You stand in the audience across from me and I keep eyeing you to see if maybe I can catch you staring at me, but every time I look in your direction you are just staring ahead, at the stage. It feels humiliating to look without being looked at. I remember all the times I loved without being loved back and that sickness is redoubled by the anticipation of having to go before you to do my little act. I bite my lip and tilt my head toward the ceiling while staring at the chandelier. I have this idea that the light will eradicate all consciousness . . . my future, whatever. I don't want to be me tonight. I want to shed the ridiculous longing.

The reading drags on and the crowd grows restless and chatty. I am placed at the very end. When it is time for me to perform, I walk onto the stage carrying Angela, my decapitated angel. Everything goes silent. Angela is wearing a red robe that is accented with gold trim. She has large white wings and there is a hole in her neck where her head is not—a bloody pit at the peak like the mouth of a volcano. She is dead but I do not know why or how she passed. Perhaps she had sinned. Perhaps she had come to Earth to dutifully protect a single human and—while dwelling amongst the basest of all sentient creatures—fell prey to worldly temptation and desire. Though I do not know her cause of death I know how to bring her back to life. I close my eyes and begin to chant elaborate incantations. The chants also narrate the resurrection process. Mystification is not part of my act. I want to be naked and to penetrate my audience with the denuded truth.

I open my eyes and look out at the crowd, then climb up a ladder and begin to blow into my decapitated angel's neck. As I blow, her blood begins to boil and bubble over.

"Ladies and genderqueers," I announced to the audience, "*a breath of life.*"

Blood starts to pool on the stage around her feet.

"If you have read The Book, you may already know the secret."

"If not," I continue, "I have shown it to you tonight."

Slowly, she comes to life.

Instead of opening doors and walking through them, I smash windows and glass walls. Everything is always locked so it has to be this way. I carry a giant ax around with me, which I stole from a fire emergency box. I worry the ax will give me away and I will be caught, but I'm not trying to be malicious . . . I simply am impatient. This mode of entering buildings goes viral. Now there are many of us who carry axes and never wait to be let in.

SURVIVOR TRAUMA

When I woke up, my back aching on a pile of clothes in the ramshackle Semiotext(e) apartment, it was hard for me to come out of the dream state.

I like the person I was in the dream.

I lived on an island that was in the path of a storm.

We all felt it coming and waited for the tsunami to swallow us.

Something inside me turned and suddenly I was brave and decisive. I began to direct the frightened ones.

I said, "When the wave comes we will close the first door, then the second. The first will break the wave's impact and the second will hold back the water.

"Then we will run to the back of the hallway and wait. When the house begins to fill with water we will leave the house through a window so we do not drown."

"Do you hear me?" I asked the frightened ones.

They were comforted by my certainty that we would survive.

But I knew that the only way to survive was to not think about whether or not we'll survive and to only do what will immediately contribute to our survival.

In the dream I was someone clear-headed and focused under pressure. The problem didn't consume me; all there was to do was solve it.

When the water came it brought a dead woman who was hysterical about the loss of her nineteenth-century daughter.

The island house was haunted by the ghost of the little girl who floated around the rooms in pea-green pajamas.

The girl had died at birth but the mother raised her ghost until the girl was old enough to move on (that is, when she reached the point at which children form memories).

The girl left. The mother was devastated.

She upbraided us for surviving.

"You think she's less real because she's a ghost?" the mother said to us with bitterness.

"She's no less real now than when she was material."

Though the girl-ghost has moved on she is alive in her mother's sadness.

WOUNDED ADJUDICATION
After Kafka

A stranger comes to my door and tells me I have to "take accountability," but refuses to name the incident for which I am to be held responsible.

Accountability?

I have heard this language before and know the whole world will be on the side of the accuser.

Language becomes an instrument for the execution of reckless adjudication

Where the pleasure of punishment is felt in common because it is righteous and no one has to answer to anyone

Where the pleasure of banishing no longer belongs to the state alone

Where there is just ban without entreaty and everyone under the spell of the language of trauma

Where anyone with a grievance can become a self-appointed judge in the name of direct democracy

Where we pretend we are just-minded and take no pleasure in punishment.

Where to speak of the relationship between pleasure and punishment would make someone a heresiarch of an unwritten anarchist code.

If we feel freed by punishment it is not because it is moral—it is the satisfaction we feel when we bring our world to equilibrium (i.e., revenge).

Nothing is corrected though there is reckoning.

Awake—have I played the accuser? Asleep—the accused?

Always, this waltz of adjudication.

In the end I am no longer able to believe that anyone is "good," though sometimes people are "correct."

Having played the wounded—maybe I needed to hear I was good

To be morally purified by the wound.

My wound becomes the Law.

My wound is too grave to be scrutinized, too heavy to speak.

It answers to no one.

Everyone will be judged through my wound.

The world will be seen through wound-colored glasses.

No, I felt no comfort in my position as judge.

Either my auto-critical impulses are too strong

Or I have never been right.

Can I even know if I did what I did for the pleasure of punishment or because my complaint was *just*?

Maybe I was equally undone by the act of admitting I had been wronged

Because to make such an assertion is a claim to dignity that goes against my primary sense of worthlessness.

The Law requires we exist.

I *become*, painfully, by condemning you.

PANIC AT THE DISCO

It is unclear to me if the flock of people and I are migrating away from the catastrophe or toward a party.

But either way—all movement is governed by something external, do we know it? The pool has rules, you can't just swim.

When someone flees is it even clear to them that they are fleeing?

The party of our life comes and goes and what remains when everything is over is a pile of things that have been left behind.

Drunk people lose shit. It is a principle of nature.

In the pile of lost things I find a lomography camera. Is it wrong for me to take it? I can't wait to develop the mysterious film.

The people who throw the party are screening Ryan Trecartin films in a warehouse that is actually the backroom of Sports Authority.

I'm not "with" everyone around me. But where am I?

Maybe I am trying to find you, then forget you, by jumping into the pool.

Yes, we are all living by three tempos: party, catastrophe, and limerence.

Sometimes tempo wires get crossed and the party feels catastrophic or the longing, a party of expectation.

We don't even know which tempo rules us—

We are just called into presence by it.

THE CHASE

A woman is trying to kill me. At first she acts friendly but then turns on me. She is spying on me. She shows Chris Kraus and Sylvère Lotringer three of my books; they are supposed to be appalled and fire me on the spot by revoking my book deal. One is HD's *HERmione* and another is Safiya Bukhari's *The War Before* . . . the third I don't remember. The books contain my marginalia. The woman stole them from me. I know I won't be able to ever relax again with her always spying on me. She is plotting all the time. She and her boyfriend are part of an ultra-leftist organization that wants to destroy us, Semiotext(e), because they consider us reformists. At times she acts helpless and when I try to help her she lashes out and tries to kill me. Yes, she is in a bathtub that is dramatically filling with water. She pretends she is drowning. I stand back, calm, but my unresponsiveness fills her with murderous rage. I don't know why she wants to kill me and turn everyone against me.

Chris Kraus and I escape on bicycles. The murderous leftist is on our trail. Then we get in a car and try to speed away . . . I believe we are in China, so everyone is driving kinda crazy. Chris is driving like a maniac, like someone in a movie who can run over everything without consequence, veering into oncoming traffic at a hundred miles per hour, leaving a trail of exploded vehicles, gushing fire hydrants, and befuddled

33

onlookers in her wake. While she is speeding through the city, she offers me a piece of pizza. I think, *What a good idea, ordering pizza. No prep. Chris is an efficient woman.* I ask her what just happened. She says the woman was trying to convince her that I am a liberal. The books are supposed to prove it. Supposedly we have lost the woman who was trying to kill us, but I get the sense that it isn't over, that she will come back for us. Sylvère is at the hotel waiting for us with another pizza. Neither of them wants to eat it, so they give the whole pie to me. The pizza is a complimentary treat that comes with the hotel room. Sylvère and Chris explain: the boyfriend of the woman is my old housemate David. This surprises me because he has always been such a nice guy, but I think that's the point—you can't trust anyone. People, reality—all unstable. Sociopaths. They'll tell you it is all a joke, everything that gets your hopes up. They are RAF-kind of leftists.

PRELIMINARY NOTES ON THE MARXIST WHITE BOY RECOGNITION SYSTEM

It is New York and I have some articles coming out in a student newspaper run by Marxist boys who believe they are the legatees of the Frankfurt School.

Their detractors think their analysis is dated and that they don't understand the nature of value under late capitalism.

The factious leftist publishers all like me. I can't understand why.

I give them my words.

We celebrate the release of *Deathnotes 3* at the editor's apartment, but a fight breaks out between the autonomists, who are of the Italian tradition, and those affiliated with French ultra-leftists such as Tiqqun.

Some insults are hurled about Negri. The communizationists cavil at his advocacy of the universal wage. Another makes a countervailing remark about the stupidity of *Theory of the Jeune Fille.*

All I can think about is escaping through drugs. Or, *I hope Kant shows up.*

Kant comes, so drugs are unnecessary.

In front of Kant I try to fake knowing and he says, "It's okay to not know everything."

I say, "What do you know better than anyone else?"

He replies, "Red Sea Turtles."

I expected him to say Emily Dickinson or Walt Whitman or pragmatist philosophy, but Red Sea Turtles is an opening.

I point to my necklace, a red turtle.

"I don't know if it's a sea turtle, but my ex-girlfriend did buy it at the aquarium."

The head falls off. It makes my rosy spirit umber with sadness.

"It's okay," I tell Kant, as though he is actually invested in the fate of the turtle on my necklace. "Now it just looks like it has retreated into its shell."

Kant asks me what subject I know better than anyone else.

I shrug and say I don't know anything.

MY DREAM ATE MY HOMEWORK

Another dream of being loved by Kant. Did he put his face against mine? I was giving a presentation on Bataille with D and one other girl. My copy of the Bataille book was all cut up. D's was intact. He was a more careful reader than I was. We showed up over an hour late, at five instead of four, and Kant said, "You never did your Bataille presentation." But we were there to do it, even though the semester was technically over. We had prepared a dance routine. I didn't remember the moves and was trying to follow along by watching the others, but my gestures were delayed. I was always lagging behind, throwing off the synchronization. D sounded like a mumbling fool. How could he be so young and balding? Nobody had any idea what he was talking about. When D finished rambling, I jumped in to save us. I said, "Bataille was a proto-surrealist who became a surrealist but was expelled from the movement by Breton, the Pope of surrealism, referred to as such because he was quick to excommunicate people from his inner circle..." As I spoke, people fell under my spell. I was like Simone Weil in *Blue of Noon*. Kant was impressed but also nervous because he didn't know who Bataille was and was afraid I would think he was stupid. He asked me questions about Bataille's work and I tried to explain *Story of the Eye*, but strained to convey how weird it was... "Little kids...an eye that is an egg that is also a bull's ball. The egg is erotic, like in the Björk music video 'Venus as a Boy.' Not exactly safe for children..." After the presentation Kant put his face against mine while the people around us partied Gatsby-style to celebrate the end of the semester.

THE MUSEUM OF CACOGRAPHY

The train is coming and all she can think to do is take a selfie to catalogue her newly missing tooth.

She goes back and forth between looking old and young, old and young—like an outdated fashion trend that circles in time to become new again. I have to strain to fix her form in place.

Things move from bad to good, bad to good between us.

I am always trying to close the distance.

Like everything in the world that doesn't know if it's young or old, she lives in the museum.

"I want to know what it's like to wake up in a museum," I tell her.

In every room of the museum there are themed parties that correspond to the objects on display.

The parties are always all around me and I volunteer to be the designated driver just to feel in relation to the crowd.

Was I unconsciously airing my crestfallenness when the woman approached me?

"You're a woman with a diseased heart," she says, "which should not be confused with heart disease, as a diseased heart is what you get after bleeding too many unstitched metaphors."

THE SEWER RAT COUNTER-HAUNTS
THE PRISON BY NESTING IN SOCIETY'S
COLLAPSING AORTA

I sneak into my brother R's prison and sleep curled up beneath the concrete, between walls, in the air vents. I'm posted up in the duct. There is always the danger of being caught by a guard.

The social structure is inside-out such that the prison is wearing its entrails. Even as a shadow-dweller I am at risk of being made into a ligament of the system. So I come with bolt cutters.

In case.

In case.

Our mother refuses to believe she has lost another child to society's dark matter: the prison. She tells herself R is younger than he is so she can think he has been locked up for fewer years.

R calls our mother to say he will not be able to file an appeal for contact visits. Though nobody sees me from my hiding place I think, *This is how they unravel families.*

Outside the prison it is always raining

As though the weather, too, were in on the conspiracy to demoralize every prisoner upon release.

Everyone who passes through the prison must also pass through the Rain of Shame.

But even this humiliating rite of passage does not guarantee release, as there is perfect symmetry between the interior and exterior of the prison. The city becomes another disc in the spine of a generalized carceral logic.

Why does the world suddenly look like the set of *Blade Runner*? But more ominous. Giant multi-story metallic blue GOOGLE BUSES hog the roads.

Though it is always raining on the destroyed city, the men of techno-science remain safe and unperturbed in their mobile metallic citadels.

Did the GOOGLE MEN make it rain on all the plebs?

Did they finally figure out how to control the weather?

DEAD LETTER DAY

You are sitting on a counter reading a letter and when you read it you start to cry.

But you say nothing and though you say nothing I know what it says.

The poet Jenny Zhang and I read the letter together.

It is printed in large Times New Roman font, double-spaced, and starts with a quote from Emily Dickinson on the beauty of dying young.

Clara killed herself by starvation for reasons not like Simone Weil. For love. Out of love for you.

Her parents sent this letter to her friends to announce her death much like someone would announce a wedding or a graduation.

But in the letter, the narcissistic parents say almost nothing about her or her death.

Concerned solely with their image as good parents, they pepper their letter with hackneyed metaphors about life, saying nothing of the corpse beneath them.

The end of the letter reads like a Wikipedia entry for a strange weather-tracking device that scientists will release into the air from South Africa.

The bundles of airborne sensors are extraordinary in that they do not seek out information.

No, they draw weather to them and convert it into mysterious data. They make weather. They have a density and magnetism that betrays their capacity for levitation.

The connection between the weather and the dead daughter is unclear.

By discussing the magical weather devices, do Clara's parents want to believe that their child's suicidal impulse was a passing storm and not part of her genuine nature? A momentary whim that was concretized and made permanent by an irreversible act?

Yet death by starvation suggests sustained deliberation—a strong will to die—and not the impetuousness of a fleetingly depressed person, who is more likely to off themselves by a gunshot to the head or pills.

The parents want to control the narrative and in doing so, deny their daughter ownership of her death.

But death robs you of release from the lovemonger's grip. I see it in the tears you shed before running off, embarrassed and emotionally exposed.

Your tears are tears of sadness but also regret.

That is, you should have been nicer to Sweetie

Though sometimes it takes someone's absence to realize what they mean to you.

(This is how the dead get revenge from the grave.)

In the dream my mother boils a mountain of frozen burritos just so she can feel sad that my little brother and I won't (*can't*) finish eating them.

THE PINK PHALLUS

Another dream that my analyst was mysteriously swapped. Who was she this time? The flaky therapist I had before her?

Did she appear in the body of my old therapist because I never see her face while on the couch?

She is the consciousness that hovers above my head.

I show up to our sessions late.

Do I travel to psychoanalysis with my friend Aimée because I am afraid to go alone?

The city has become smart. A smart apartment building has just been built. My analyst's practice moves to the Cybernetic Tower of Commerce.

But the cybernetic smart city is so complicated and unpredictable that I always arrive late.

Ryan and I live in the same city again. I try to take a photo of the books a homeless man gave me for free: Gide, Varda, Céline, Rimbaud.

He is the man who died after giving Kalan a book about black holes . . .

I tell my analyst that the secret to being cured is the feminist commune, that life will be fixed if I can live with my friends.

How did I get to this recently deindustrialized Caribbean island?

And why, when industry leaves a city, does it look like a bomb has gone off?

All that remains of the glory days is the ghostly presence of hollowed machines.

The driver gives me a tour. "Only one pallet of the famous mulch we produced for years is left."

How strange, this guide: a keeper of declension. One man survives to tell the story of the island's fall.

There are no other people on the island any longer.

I look up. There is an abandoned hotel towering above, now just a shell of a building. (The Divine Loraine?)

A destroyed pink tower. A monument to mobile commerce.

A priapic shaft that splits the sky like a cut.

Ah but there are young people willing to inhabit the ruin.

To channel their immense energy into terraforming the wreck.

The party queers of New College arrive to throw flamboyant gatherings in the abandoned pink phallus.

They spray-paint neon stripes on their white clothing and dance until the island comes back to life.

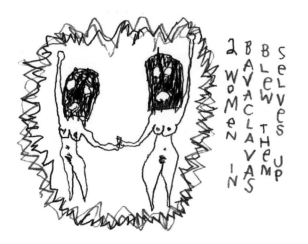

2 WOMEN IN BAVACLAVAS BLEW THEM SELVES UP

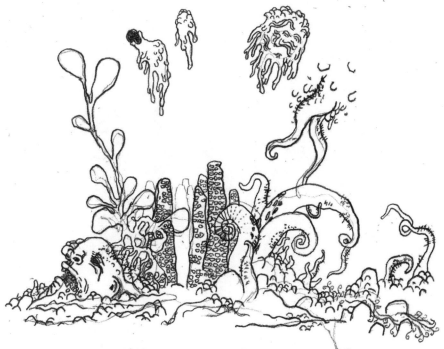

everything mutated & cancerous

Feminist Gommune

AN INVENTORY OF ONEIROGENIC HERBS AND SUBSTANCES

Silene Capensis (African dream herb)

Calea Zacatechichi (Oaxacan dream herb)

Mugwort

Entada Rheedii

Magnesium

Syrian Rue

5-HTP

Vitamin B6

Melatonin

Galantamine + Choline

AN INVENTORY OF SCENES FROM ONEIROGENIC HERB DREAMS

The blood clot on the floor

Guarding the door, trying to protect the blood clot

Screaming GET OUT to the person trying to come into the bathroom

Not having a tampon

Blood dripping down my leg

The window and its terrible translucency

The police officer outside the window

The man outside the window discussing my fate with his accomplices

The decapitated angel, Angela

Resuscitating the decapitated angel by blowing into her neck

bell hooks lost in the glass aviary

A bell lost in the birds

The mottled crustaceans Clutch dumped onto the wood floor

And offered to me as a psychedelic drug

Always, the movie theater interior of the airplane

The rush through the city to the airport

The man who suddenly appears while we are rushing

He is holding us back and we almost don't make it

Poems scrolling on the aquarium glass

Wanting to hug you on the shore

Breaking the shell when I was just trying to clean it off

Feeling terrible about breaking the shell

Everything here is fragile

The town where it is always Christmas

The women parading and preening in full plumage

The end of the road and the beginning of the dirt field

C's mother debating the decision to become either a psychoanalyst or bed and breakfast owner

Social anxiety at AWP and the craving for valium

The vaudevillian family and the bratty girl I was forced to tutor in piano

All the dreams where I am spoken to in Chinese and I can't speak back

The falling bridge of language

The pyramid covered in fake flowers

Accidentally destroying the flowering pyramid, somebody's gift

Falling down the deep rift in the stone

The limestone rocks that tumbled with me

The disturbing faces in the rocks covered with moss

The girl trapped in the house with the doctor and her mother, the tyrant

Riding a wooden horse through the night with LaKeyma, on a mission to release the girl

The mighty datura vine and my fear of its power

A night imbued with evil

Trying to stop S from riding her scooter because I am afraid she will die

Fucking Cindy in a geodesic dome that I built by hand

During sex Cindy turns into a man who makes fun of me

And Nosh tells me how I can bring power to my dome

Falling asleep with Elaine in the ashes of a fire pit

The glass buildings and the bridge that leads to Egypt

The torso stuffed with green beans

The people making Halloween decorations

The desire to kiss S and the fear

Settling for kissing his neck instead

Falling asleep in the library only to wake up to find I have completed nothing

And there is so much to do

My father waiting in the parking lot

He comes to me so we can complete the Lego mountain range

But before we finish the building begins to flood

We're on the second floor and the water is rising

I suggest we use the fire escape so we won't drown

I want him to be proud of me

THE COVERT APOCALYPSE

We're all the contemplatives of an ongoing apocalypse.
Etel Adnan

A guilt dream unlike any other guilt dream I've experienced before. The world was ending.

I woke up to my father crying in a way I've never seen him cry before. He could not accept our collective fate.

Everything was mutated and cancerous. He was stubborn and kept radioactive material around because he couldn't throw it away.

I had to yell at him, "DAD. LET IT GO. You'll poison us all this way." He broke down crying, unable to accept reality.

He had a tin of coffee. I told him he had to throw it away immediately, that anything metal was highly radioactive.

My aunt had become feeble and diseased. It pained me to see a powerful woman so weak. She became mortal to me for the first time.

What was the apocalyptic disease? That Thing, I know it when I see it. The masses were being sent to their deaths by Harvard.

The death march looked like a ceremony, like a graduation. I knew who was going to die, who was diseased and possessed by The Thing.

I saw a woman with a broken sandal and knew she would die, unable to keep *IT* out.

I knew that if I marched with the crowd I would die too, so I fled. I hid in the stairwell of a Harvard building.

Who was the man I called to save me? It must have been Dylan. Did he know telepathically?

I'm jumping around in time because of how jarring my father's tears were when I woke up. Did my mother die when The Thing broke out?

The marching people were physically deformed by The Thing, yet no one acknowledged it.

Everyone denied the existence of the apocalyptic disease.

It was gaslighting on a broad scale. I had to fight so hard to hold on to my reality. Everyone was trying to convince me it was all okay.

I felt guilty about surviving, what I had to do to survive. To avoid catching the disease, I had to leave behind those who had contracted it.

It was impossible to tell people what they wanted to hear. I felt terrible, disappointing everyone with the truth. That's why I was in hiding for so long . . .

An administrator almost caught me. Was he a carrier too? His gaze forced me out of hiding. It was then that I fled . . .

That's when Dylan came with the car. The carriers were all chasing me . . .

Yes the man who saved me in the dream was like the man who saved the undutiful daughter in the Turkish film *Mustang*.

What are the lost parts of the dream? God, how alone it felt to be fighting for myself against the world.

What was my analyst doing in the dream? I had a feeling she was not diseased. She appeared as the physical embodiment of the Law.

In the dream she tells me to go to the courthouse to defend Roe v. Wade, which is under attack. She has become a high-profile lawyer.

Did it pain me to see that my analyst had other patients . . . other "students"?

I must have ignored her injunction to go to the Supreme Court—not out of a desire to disobey, but to avoid the plague.

How terrible it is to tell the hoarding father that he has to let go.

How awful I felt looking at my feeble father clutching his paltry tin of coffee grounds.

Did his hands shake?

We had nothing.

He, destroyed.

SOWERS OF DISCORD

There is a bombing that disrupts the religious ceremony.

I have just become Jewish by marrying into a Jewish family.

Two women in balaclavas blow themselves up. There is a deafening sound, confetti, chaos . . .

The people at the religious service cannot understand their motivations.

The women had been asked to sing. They refused.

Resources have not been equitably distributed. Their disruption is a form of protest on behalf of the disaffected women of the world— feminist killjoys, smile defectors, and other saucy spoilsports.

The women do not die. After the explosion, they run. They are giddy with outlaw jouissance. Everyone else, fear-stricken.

Afterward people debate the morality of their intervention, everyone vying for a claim to the position of biggest Victim.

Should I reunite with my family?

Does it exhaust me?

CUNT RIVER

Internal light always provides anyone who consults it a clear response.
Simone Weil

My friend is on MDMA and when we walk through Sears for her amusement, there is a throng of gay boys in fast food uniforms making out.

She starts to cry.

She says I'm not paying attention to her.

She says I am too busy watching TV.

I wasn't looking at the TV.

I was looking above the TV, at a four-foot tall painted book of my friend Joohyun's poetry.

Joohyun had spread thick blue paint on a canvas and with her finger wrote a poem about a cunt and a river.

I knew that she was just one of many sad women who have transubstantiated their limerence into beautiful, self-assured poetry painted viscerally on giant canvases.

They become luminous this way.

To turn oneself again toward the sun is an act of faith.

HÉLÈNE CIXOUS

A DIFFICULT APPRENTICESHIP

They

say

young sun

flowers turn toward

the sun even in the

absence of sun, do you remember the imperiled

sunflower at the end of the world, when he burned all his light—

how long did you keep turning, did you kneel with your palms out as

Clytie forever in a pose of supplication?

The town half underwater. The colorful adobe houses lining the shore and the waves that are about to swallow them. You are excited to show me things I haven't seen before: the ocean hidden beneath the scorched Earth and the island village that will soon be underwater. While we are talking to the old man, who is the custodian of the island, he gestures toward the looming waves as he speaks about what will soon be lost.

But is it ocean? How, in the desert—but this was underwater once: mollusk remains litter the hills. Again, the dream of finding a secret body of water. You show it to me. You are trying to drive me home, but I am too delirious with longing to direct you and that's how we end up at the water. Do your parents live in the threatened village? In the town everyone has a job but it doesn't always run smoothly because not everyone does their job. Your parents are the people from the post office. I take a shower at their house and hear them talking about how uncouth I am. Did I forget to take off my shoes? I think you hear, do you hear them say, What's wrong with her, she was perfectly polite when she lived with us. *And somehow I know you will rise to my defense.*

When I finish the humiliating shower you are outside leaning against your white truck. I feel bad about keeping you waiting but you are nice about it, say you will drive me home. On the way, we stop at a shopping mall. In the center of the parking lot is a slot machine you cannot resist. You want to put $82 into the machine. It is night. I tell you to play 75 and keep your remaining 7. The machine spits out some tickets. While redeeming your arcade prize you lean in to whisper something into my ear and though I do not hear it, I know.

Your body folds. You collapse beneath the weight of your love. D whispers, Is he okay, *as I hold you in my arms, or are you holding me? I feel you becoming weak as the vendor stands watching us from behind the counter, waiting for you to select your prize. What is this moment, the warmth emanating from you? Still limp and in a trance you strain to whisper something about wanting the book by the Asian woman called Sunflower. The cover of the book is red and dark magenta. You are slow to come to consciousness but the first thing you do is mumble: the sunflower book. It is code for love.*

Did I take another shower at the bookman's house? Somehow I end up in your class and am anxious because I haven't done the reading. But I am in luck. The reading is Bachmann's Malina—*but who are you?*

What

is

the distance

between tournesol and

turnsole, a whole mythology erected

on a false recognition, what I saw when

       I ran your blog through Google Translate: entries peppered with
                                       references to Kafka

       and Jung's *Red Book*, spelunking as auto-analysis. You posted a
                 picture of a foil-wrapped burrito. I thought you had

written

something

profound. My

Slavic Studies friend

informed me that you purchased

a potato, having mistaken it for a burrito.

Many suns revolve in the void: to all that is dark they speak with their light—to me they are silent. Oh, this is the enmity of the light against what shines: merciless it moves in its orbit. Unjust in its heart against all that shines, cold against suns—thus moves every sun.

The suns fly like a storm in their orbits: that is their motion. They follow their inexorable will: that is their coldness.

Oh, it is only you, you dark ones, you nocturnal ones, who create warmth out of that which shines. It is only you who drink milk and refreshment out of the udders of light.

FRIEDRICH NIETZSCHE

The Sun Will BE our
Last Song

WHY GRIEVING PEOPLE
ARE DRAWN TO WATER

I.

Right after you left
I had the same dream.
We were back at the lake.

I ask you not to let me face the water, for water is the only one who knows what has always been. On opposite sides of the lake we stand not facing the water, separately dreaming the same dream. Your father has just died and I am trying to be there for you. We are at the house I grew up in. You start to walk toward the lake and I follow you. It is the lake I would walk to barefoot at sunrise when I couldn't fall asleep as a teenager. To get to the lake we have to cut through the cranky woman's yard. I know she is somewhere in her garden watering her plants, hiding behind a shrub while she watches us amble across her lawn, shooting us the evil eye. We are immune to her diabolical glare. Her lawn ornaments and garish garden statues are obstacles placed to make us stumble as we push toward the lake. I have the feeling she is calling the cops on us so I am anxious to reach the fence.

As we walk up to the lake the water unhooks itself and starts to swell, grain by grain, until it is no longer lake, but ocean.

HOW THE EGG LOSES ITS SHAPE

II.

It could have been
Ashfield Lake
or a tributary
of the Connecticut River.

We are on the shore of something continental. I want to give you a hug but I can't—an invisible force holds me back. I know that if I try to hold you, you will turn to dust. Everything is very fragile. I pick up a seashell that is covered in sand and thick green goo. My instinct is to peel the goo off the shell so I can uncover its true form, but the shell breaks as I try to clean it with my finger. I look down at what I am holding and see the hole in her hide. Feel so sick. I don't understand what has changed but I know I will never be able to touch you again.

DAMNATION

III.

We were floated out on pink waves, the
thundering floorboards spilling the silence of
your bewildered face, the face I knew
was without the face it takes to remember,

> The bed is waiting for us
> Unmade
> And the flooded street
> Will let us go

But if you'll only make it halfway
—I'll go through it with you
carry my calendula salve to Hell
to rub into your sunburned
membrane, remembering, I was
there with you in the sun
touching your hand with my pinky
just so you'd know who I am
that *I am*

When I touched your hand you
looked up at the sky and said,

This sun will be our last song
It will come loud and crazy
bathing our arms in
unbearable ringlets of light
and the light will be
the break you will call
the only prayer intoned
to wake you from the nightmare

WILLOW SISTERS

We didn't know when it was safe to stop waiting, so we just kept waiting.

At night the sisters laughed beneath the willow tree. By the next day they were part of the landscape.

We dance beneath the skirt of the willow. We sing because we know what it feels like to think—We are going to die. We know because we look up at the sky and the stars burst into clamorous sermon.

"One voice at a time! We can only understand one voice at a time."

Sometimes I feel it, there is a mirror in a place I cannot see
lights flashing outside my window behind my head

you gave me   a mouth
so I could hide   my nightmare
from the man   outside my window

Get away from the glass opening.

The man is coming.

They hide in the dirt and listen as he approaches, the dead leaves cracking beneath his boots. They synchronize their breaths with the tempo of his stride.

We see it. The dead trunk stands tall against the sky and we remember that we are alone and fatherless.

Sometimes when you are afraid you pretend you are talking to your mother:

Call me little lentil, sweet pea, mom I love when you call me a tender legume.

There is death hiding in these branches   and no way to know.
But father will know.

My father   *wake up*   gasping   what his daughter has just seen.
His daughter cannot die before he does.

For once, night will end. The wind blows the leaves off of the pecan trees as we walk past the flooded grove.

With their lanterns they walked to see the river
and a single word   released   floats down the stream.

Their consolation was formalized. Everyone who saw the word was brought to consolation.

Beside the grove-shore they knelt and watched thousands of pouched leaves set sail for the night.

We want to know: is this the end? It is the first thing that has ever felt real.

For the first time the unwritten book that lives in my stanza was permitted to take over. Blood dripped down my leg as the voices played. Suddenly I couldn't remember if it was a dream, if I really swam in a tank full of sharks as my little brother stood on the steps, afraid to enter the water.

Let her remember   she was part of that world.
She saw the plaid bedspread turn into a worm and crawl toward her.
The whole world was contained in the way the worm moved.

She saw the girls dried up in the dirt, peeled for the conscience of everyone not dead.

Their bodies, dried beyond recognition. They had to be identified by their teeth.

The first time we came to the willow tree to play, a man was there, beneath the awning, sitting cross-legged in the grass. This man became a role model for us simply because he sat beneath the tree and let himself feel tired. Not you. He is not you who have spilled this many words because you couldn't let yourself tire.

Once I was ill and I thought about calling you. I wanted to give you a tour of what I had seen, to tell you

> *This is where the nightmare happened*
> *and this is where I hid.*

You are standing outside the house because you don't want to have this conversation around people. Your phone is about to die.

The last thing I say . . . I don't even know if you heard it. I said, "I know I am with you as a character but not as a person." And then I realized you were no longer there. I saw you holding your dead phone while you walked up the driveway, wiping your tears. I knew you were gone long before your voice cut out.

Nobody knows where we've been. It's true we never asked them to know but we wanted them to at least try to understand: there are many people in this world who want to hurt us.

I saw her scab peeled and beneath it, something terrible. A terrible loneliness in her re-opened wound.

We speak to you from nowhere   and sing because we are alone.

I walked through the trees and it was so dark I could not see what waited for me at the end of the path. Animal shrieks sliced the shadows. Beneath the skirt of the willow tree I stood laughing to myself. I liked to remember myself like this, laughing beneath the willow. But I could not stay there forever. So I walked.

And there, in an irrigation ditch, two dried up bodies still holding hands.

In the face of the stone
two faces in the stone

The faces of the two
who died simply because
they knew
                    We will die.

WHAT WILL YOU EAT?

It was like everything in the world had a place, you said, and nobody questioned where they were.

And from our spots not askance

We were patient

We waited till the end of the night to eat our cucumber

Because only when it was over could we declare

This is ours

And skin our game and halve

Then halve the half and pass it leftward to be shared

At the end of the night a phone call from CoCo—*who is CoCo?*—she only speaks Chinese. When she opens her mouth and begins to talk, my brain shuts off. I never want to hear Chinese again. Don't test me! I cry in nightmares. Once I asked my father to speak to me in Chinese and he said, "Ni xihuan xigua ma?" *Do you like watermelon?* At that the language unwound and built itself, stroke by stroke, around this condition, melon, of which the cucumber belongs.

We ate the word then fell asleep.

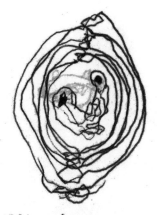

MAKING SWEET LOVE
INSIDE OUR LITTLE
POCKET OF THE VOID

IM   A BODY OF ANGELS ALL OF ME

Rice cooker   LASeRJet PRiNter

all alone and fatherless*~.

HOW TO SHED THE WORLD

A woman comes to the class inside the theater bearing flowers, a critique of femininity. There are many floors. You have to take a mystical elevator to get to the theater in the sky. All I want is to abscond with my lover. There is a hotel room and before entering I say, "We have to shed our connection to the world." At the threshold we leave our phones, computers—everything that binds us to the world so that inside the room it will be . . . just us.

A strange abyss. The abyss you face when you no longer exist for the digital world. We feel anxious at first but then sink into that nothingness, making sweet love inside our little pocket of the void. I am becoming a wolf. I have shaved my entire body to be more feminine but the hair grows back thicker and longer than before. Long fur is growing on my back. Did I develop hirsutism when I stopped eating? The hair on my back is so long I can make a Mohawk with it. At some point I leave the room to look for food. All the prepared food at the grocery store is gone but near where the sushi should be is a rare Ancient Greek soda covered with pink flowers. Later I realize the bottle is already half empty and leave it in the deli, where there is a shelf of free music on CDs, tapes and vinyl: a public archive of lost sounds. I miss music so

I go to see what the deli has to offer. Most of it is bad (except Mates of State), but what is on the mysterious unmarked tapes?

In the theater I do performances and speak to the class about prisons. Noise music kids are in attendance. But it is the smell of the flower that changes everything—a sprig of Jasmine? The secret knowledge of flowers. Something familiar . . .

THE PHANTASMAGORIA OF FAILURE

In the dream, the feeling of being publicly effaced. I was doing an improv performance and was struggling to engage the audience. An older woman who was much more established and powerful than me started taking over my show. She had to control everything to ensure I would not upstage her and that my performance would flop. Every time I started, she shot down what I did. Now, too timid to begin, the audience began my pieces for me using my instructional annotations. There was a simple melody I had written that a man began to play on a piano. A girl in the audience began to sing the warbling anthem for lost souls and I started to harmonize with her. When I sang I would start soft, then my voice would gather energy and shatter the bell jar hemming me in; the emotion would rise, the form would unwind, from a whisper to a bellow there was just a pure feeling I tried to channel for the purpose of transporting the audience. When I finally began to find my rhythm, the controlling woman would not let me go there. She stopped the show in the middle of the piece, claiming I had gone on for too long. I felt humiliated. Had I lost track of the time while dawdling and gone on for hours? The show ended before the orgasmic energies that had been quietly gathering could erupt. Sensing my defeat, the girl who sang during the performance tried to reassure me that the performance was great. She was a fan and longtime follower of my work. I knew she was a fellow lost-girl when I heard her speak another language to her mother, for it indicated she had been *transplanted*.

How did we end up in the aisle of a dark bike shop testing fireworks? I was looking for new ways to create an otherworldly atmosphere during my performances and came up with: blue smoke. A man tried to sell me incense sticks that release blue smoke, but the sticks were attached to smoke bombs I believed would explode. We tested the blue smoke in the bike shop. Since it was dark I could hardly see anything. Outside, the sun had almost set on the garage of dashed dreams. I walked, in a fading sliver of light, still thinking about the failed performance, dwelling on the thought that whatever it was I wanted to send did not send.

CREATURES ABANDONED BY TIME

Everyone wants to be how they are not
Everyone believes they are who they are not

I took a break from my blog only to direct all my energy into journaling

Notebooks fill up

You can't imagine how much attention I give the worm on the sidewalk
   of LA
or the tree of coral inside my dream

Because I don't know how to be in the world
I don't know how to write toward you

I remember how devotional I felt the morning
the cottonwoods released their seeds to the wind
The way the morning mysteries formed the backdrop of my sadness

Disjunction between inner and outer worlds
meet in an equivalence of language

Experience completes me, I think, and that is dangerous
It loses me there: in the depths of cosmic rays

Long enough to clarify milky images of cotton and moon and
seeds enshrined in threads of pure flight

The dream of transmuted longing, a tickled clitoris

I'm a body of angels, all of me
In the space of what is possible when injured and in need

Something personal permitted by the friend who hears
Who is drawn by the gravity of the wound
Toward the center of the sky that sleeps between my ribcage

What gift?

On the arc of deviation:
a parabola of attention
I learn

I am always entering the dome
in search of a vision beyond the corridor
A way to calculate the slope of your ascent
When you walk up the stairs
Leaking memory

At the top is where it pools and I am amazed
Because when I look through it my gaze turns this disorder
into an architecture of comprehension

The fig on the tree in Mexico
is sweet and I always
get attached to a specific cup

Creatures abandoned by time
A note that says,
"All I remember is an ocean that was too cold for me"

Near the shore a boy and his father pull
a hard thing out of a large clump of seaweed

A stone
A dream of the way your energy wanes
when nobody is paying attention

HOW TO MEASURE USE VALUE

Cindy L was driving drunk. Creepy men were trying to sell us a gray puppy in the shadows. There were carnival lights in the distance. Carrie was on the celebratory bridge doing her usual Internet thing but under a different avatar. I remember . . . there was a straw that was a slide into Canada. Did you have to shrink to go through it? I almost got stuck. I almost drowned. The water was refreshing . . . so cold you felt clean. It was night but the pawn shops were still open. Someone was selling a rice cooker. *A very useful appliance*, I thought. *Perhaps the most useful of them all*. But I didn't buy it. Instead I bought a LaserJet printer and tested it out. I could feel my book come into being. Who were the people trying to sell us things? A man was fiddling with his broken iPhone. Is that case new? *No*, he said. *I've had it a while.*

WAITING FOR GODEL

First of all nobody will survive money.

Of course I understand this poem and by that I mean I understand what it means to be a disappeared writer who wakes to tinnitus like all my life is this morning tinnitus because the soundtrack to my life is exhaustion whereas those subalpine I mean sibylline those sumptuous beauts of the celestial order have got a kinder aural factory atmosphere symphony factory to make the day leap with a plangent start.

A dream comes to me and I am in a classroom being tested. No one is present to administer the test—I must be here to test myself. (We know how that will go.) What makes this dream interesting is that I am waiting for someone I do not know (i.e. a stranger). And then I'm outside in the desert and it's cold it's a vacant rodeo and I'm still waiting. Approach, already!

Who said: is this woman of color ontology—this waiting—Debbie knows and loves the poem of waiting, and all great poems of waiting—Tennyson's COME INTO THE GARDEN MAUD—which may or may not be a poem of waiting though we did have to wait to look it up on the computer. Between remembrance and re-enactment: there is waiting.

But I truly believe we're not waiting to become our better selves, that we're already so great as it is. We are aureoled beings doing our being thing

It's not easy being alive

This I know

But sometimes the moon is such that you just kind of slide into the glory hole that is your life, the brave freewheeling musicality of existence.

THE DEATH OF THURSTON MOORE

It's funny the way the moment becomes its own world. I can't even enter the worlds that once housed me. The memory. My memory? I thought it was mine but now it excludes me. The truth of the moment becomes a truth that is almost impossible to access once it has passed. But it is also insoluble. That comforts me, to know that what happened will always have happened, that the event is immiscible.

Keeled over in a giant pile of clothes at the foot of my bed—I remembered: the truth of the moment. It was after I had gotten back from Massachusetts. A music track I made for a poem came on and suddenly I was transported to my last poetry reading. Thurston Moore was in the audience so he became my temporal reference point. I wondered what I transmitted to him in that moment, though I knew that whatever it was, it would not last. I'm okay with that. Thurston Moore was my reference point because I received transmissions from him as early as middle school, when I bought my first Sonic Youth CD. See he doesn't even know that his *Daydream Nation* emissions touch the hearts of adolescent girl-rockers who grow up to be fierce poets. (Though I was never a SY fangirl—I was more of a Joy Division kind of girl.) After the reading I wrote a private essay about being a middle school rocker, loving music so fucking much, wanting to be a music journalist and watching *Almost Famous* with my dad. During the film he said, *That's you!* Rock kid journalist. I did actually interview bands. The night after the reading I had a dream about Thurston Moore.

I dreamed of bereavement. The Chinese were spying on us, their helicopters flying sideways outside our window to get a better view. (Not very subtle of them.) No doubt my unconscious was inculcated with the Cold War-style neo-yellow peril I had absorbed from reading the *New York Times* every day. I was supposed to fight in a war but was too afraid to die. In Chinese, I asked the women in the cafeteria what was happening and—insulted by the mockery I made of their native tongue—they replied in irate English. I was with my friends and lovers in a building and it started to collapse. There was the horror of impending death, but what happened was worse than death—everyone died except me, including my husband Thurston Moore. I was beside myself with grief, and it didn't help that there was Sonic Youth merchandise EVERYWHERE I went.

What was the meaning of the dream? I think that Thurston Moore was not Thurston Moore at all, that he was a cipher, that the death of Thurston Moore was actually the death of my youth—dare I say it, the loss of my *sonic youth*? Once a wide-eyed rocker, now a domesticated writer! Nat said, *When I saw you read poetry for the first time, you seemed like such a rock star.* It didn't seem like he was talking about me. I was always the fan.

NOBODY WILL
SURVIVE MONEY

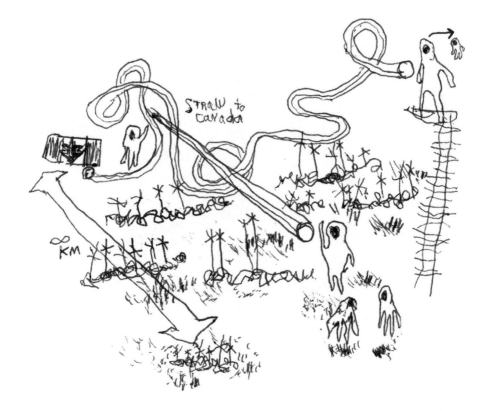

STRAW to
Canada

∞KM

we were just ordooolod BEINGS DOING OUR BEING thing

CREATION STORY

You were in my dream in the body of a hardcore guy from my past; I cannot quite place him maybe an Underoath member or something. You sat across the table from me at psychoanalysis, not saying anything, just staring, and my analyst was confused. *Is this couples therapy?* No, I said, I barely know this person.

I woke up while I was dangling from a floating whoopee cushion that was dragging me across a field. The farting device was worth thousands, perhaps millions, of dollars. My friend's girlfriend was cosmic belly dancing for a throng of gawking white men while half-speaking Spanish and playing with rubber chickens.

Maybe you should illustrate my dream book.

DREAMING IN PAPYRUS

Two days after my grandma died I dreamed my friend Leah had stolen the first book of oneiromancy, *The Ramesside*, an Egyptian dream book housed at the British Museum. The papyrus became another substance in her possession. I woke thinking that the British Empire can never own the dream, only its "residue"—the artifact: the material on which the prophecy is inscribed, not the prophecy itself. Much was missing. I thought of Anne Carson's translation of Sappho where brackets appear in the poems where the papyrus has disintegrated, as papyrus is the structure of dreams. Never intact. Always half-dissolved. I don't remember what Leah and I did with the book of dream interpretation, just that a retinue of doting young suitors followed me around campus and my academic adviser had to teach them how to love me.

THE CORAL TREE

I have been having such strange and beautiful dreams lately, though I was only able to sleep for a couple hours last night. I dreamed I was walking through a bombed-out abandoned building . . . just a shell of a building, really; there were no windows or doors and it was quite dark. But right outside one of the doorways there was a luminous tree—not just any tree but a coral tree—not just the color coral but the stony sea substance—and this radiant tree was growing up out of a little pond that shimmered in the light—and instead of leaves it was covered in delicate glass threads—everything was very bright and I knew that as soon as I exited the dilapidated building and passed through the doorway, the world would really open up, kind of like that rush you get in the morning when you step out of your house and into the sunlight. I write this because . . . maybe I am thinking of what Michael Hardt says about the imagination being constitutive, the way the imagination "becomes so intense and embedded that it becomes real through its intensification and articulation." So I think . . . these flashes of the luminous world should be shared. I don't believe the imagination can fix everything (I am a rigorous materialist!), but it can do some of the work: the work of creating openings where there were previously none. In my talk on revolutionary loneliness I reminded the audience that how we choose to interpret life and death is not neutral; interpretation itself is always strategic. Some interpretations are more politically and personally enabling than others. I think of this when I write my dreams down in the morning. When I had this dream I thought, *Here is the destroyed world, and here—beyond the threshold—is the luminous world.* Simone Weil says that the greatest calamity the human race can experience is the *destruction of a city.* That's where I was: walking through a destroyed city. But . . . the luminous tree!

THE STORM

What did I want? To be loved by X? But X won't come near me when the lights go off. Someone is mad and the plug of a Chinese electronic keeps falling out of the socket. My voice changes. I say, *Do you remember who I am? It's me, Jackie. Do you even know who I am?* Why do I believe you don't remember? Again, the world has lost its object constancy. I have to explain all over again that my brother is still in prison. And they say, *Still?* Because they've forgotten. Because it's no longer an event. I am always just "crashing" at a friend's house, hoping to be touched. Where is E? She's Airbnb-ing a house on a river. Is this supposed to be the Hudson River? Can I stay with you?

There is a map inside my mind of all the destroyed bridges. Some time ago, there was a storm. The aftermath replays in real-time. I am showing the friend-turned-stranger my memories like Žižek guiding you through cinema. The people are running. I am wading through the water. But is that me? Can you tell me, is she me? (The one who is escaping.) My old best friend Crystal is running in her Kash n' Karry grocery store work uniform. I tell him, *That's my old best friend Crystal. We worked together at a grocery store in a Florida town called Holiday.* Then I see the bridge fall apart. People are falling into the water and getting dragged off by the current. The couple starts to argue about which bridge it is. We look at our mental map together, dragging the topography telepathically with our neural lace appendage, like Google Maps of the future. *Here. This is where the destruction happened.* Suddenly I am dizzy because I'm not where I think I am. They point to an estuary near a Great Lake. How did I get here? How do I not know where I am? I called everyone I could think of and asked if I could stay with them. I waited. I went where I was permitted to go. Am I in the Midwest? I thought this was New York. But the world is such that the Midwest and New York are the same thing, as the storm compresses space and collapses the distance through geographic folding.

What is it about the building that makes it like the edifice of a grocery store? There are piles of wood on the crumbling bridge and then I am sad at the point in the night when I realize X won't cuddle me. Later there is a group of boys standing outside, all wearing tie-dye shirts because it's their "uniform." Do I feel left out?

the body vernacular

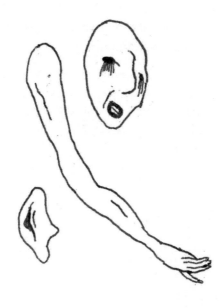

BEING IS WITHOUT SHELTER

Do you know what it's like to sleepwalk through the arid dreamscape of nowhere to go?

I turn to face the battered gorge

There is breath in the crease

Sleep there

When it's time

Someone will wake you and lead you across the desert to where the ceremony awaits you

In the glorious cascade of brightly colored paper

This was made for you

The half-formed piñata of yesterday's dream

They won't forget you anymore

Be a little open, will you

To the love that wants to be your coat

So I walk to where you can't see me

I can see you

Through the crack in the wall

There is fright in your cheek

The sensation of being watched

There's a little burning in your nose

A fear-lash falling like a feather from the Ferris wheel

Do you remember how terrible—

The light shining on our weakness.

In the Utah desert with nowhere to hide

We were so unlucky when it came to forgetting

We didn't know how to, had nowhere to store our stones

Our ribs got a little bent out of shape

MASOCHISM OF THE KNEES

Who is the girl forced to kneel on dried chickpeas to atone for the sin of being alive?

In the dream blindfold and bandage are one.

My hands go numb as I carry dried chickpeas.

In my head there is a voice that says "naked forest" and

"a tiny photograph that is passed between hands in the dark."

Why doesn't the girl on the floor of the world talk?

Because she's a wound on the earth's hide.

Not mouth.

Do you understand?

Wound, not mouth.

FUCKING ON THE COW

I sent her a text saying, I just dreamed we had sex.

She said, *I hope you liked it as much as I did.*

Somehow I feel this has happened before?

I said, the dream? Yes. Once we did it on a cow with giant udders. This time you had a penis and I was covered in rust. We were in a house that I owned and the bed that once belonged to your father was always made...

candles were always lit. (It was an image of devotion.) E was making bright blue beef jerky in a nearby house while F slept.

(Always, the dream of fucking my friend and suddenly, she has a penis. Sometimes I start bleeding. Sometimes I bleed all over the floor. Sometimes the Plath-girl who snorted coke off the table comes and strikes a fistful of matches against the wall. Sometimes I am stuck in a loop, and she will not stop striking the matches against the wall.)

WHAT DID SHE WANT TO PROVE?

We were in the cabin. I started making out with you on your bed and then I kissed between your breasts. We started rubbing and touching. You had a big clit or a little penis and I could feel it through my pants as you rubbed against me. You pushed your inscrutable girl-member between my legs. When you were working me up I remembered I was on my period, so I pulled away to change my tampon. In the bathroom I realized there were no tampons, only dollar-store panty liners. I knew the blood would spill and it did; it dripped down my leg like the first time I fucked my ex-girlfriend. Was another girl making out with you when I returned? Did we all start making out?

Was the girl who joined us the girl I asked on a date when I was 21—the Plath-girl who snorted coke off her dorm room desk while talking about hating everything except animals? Was she burning yellow matches, striking them against the wall?
Did she explain why they kept breaking?
Did she notice that they were breaking?
Did she break the match?
Did she strike the match?
Did she break the match by striking the match?

Did the heads of the matches fall off?
Was there yellow phosphorus smeared on the white wall?
Did their heads fall off?
Was there fire?
Did she burn her fingers?
Did their heads fall off?
Why was she showing us?
Did the people gather to watch her strike the matches against the wall?
Did their groins burn while they watched?
Did they feel the heat in their bodies?
Were they afraid of the heat?
Did she want us to look?
Why did she want us to look?
Did she want to prove that she was a woman of the flame?
Did she burn her fingers trying to show us the fire?

Bataille says the phosphorus content of a "normal man"
Would make 2200 matches
And that his fat would make seven cakes of soap.

I keep looking at the yellow smear on the wall.

BECAUSE THERE IS SILENCE

On the way to the light the tree fell onto the gravel
In the paper cut, a downward sensation lands in the garden of
    wandering wounds
I am alone in this Chicago garden, on a bench eating candy and
    a banana
A symphony of rats becomes the echo of a text written by the one
    who does not belong anywhere
The "voice of exile," Du Bois said of the sorrow songs
Of people outside time, without ground

Where am I, in all this—in the chaos of a city that moves
    without thinking
All day I struggle to make a day
Bury myself in sand and dust
And from nowhere sing that the tolling bell is for us, our rebirth

The plaintive knell of premature departure is inside me
What you'll find:
The opened book of our birth
Knowledge of where we are on this earth

There is nothing to do but take the book with us wherever we go

It is a heavy book

Through it you know your station and what you will find

Let me sleep let me sleep I write to find—
To know—
I mean I write to—
It is the bloodletting of the self
In the stutter
When there is nothing to say
Just a desert of language that unfurls before a pure mystical feeling

"I" is the background of thought at the beginning of sleep
Or the fog that surrounds you like the awareness of death when you
    face the corpse

How many ways can we be killed by what we made for ourselves when
    we felt weak?

They say, "You're undermining yourself"
"You make the impossible mountain just to weep at its feet"
As if you didn't know that you've traded your chance at a propitious
    "I" for a few hours of eyeless repose

Some have faith at the end of their failure
But you are always looking for a reason to give up

The fog is your way of remembering to forget the three centipedes
     in your closet
Look at the distressed face of the baby held by the priest in the giant
     mural
You say, *I love the parts of you I cannot assimilate*, but there's nothing
     innovative about the way you say it

When I don't feel bad about myself Kant's importance shrinks

Like the banks I merge to become something greater than myself
A plough made from the steel of melted swords
Or a chariot made from the flesh of 600 melted angels

What constitutes this—this lack of formation, when all my thoughts
pool to reflect you—in or on the surface of the sound of the lesbian
bass player piercing the accelerando hearts of 600 teens drunk on the
possibility of being seen while lost in *it*.

My ears are still ringing.

The dyke has charcoal around her eyes, everyone is singing and
sometimes I'm in a funny mood—laconic like H.D.'s *HERmione*, who
sees the corner of a piece of fabric but not the event—not the primary
matter of what has passed between us.

How can someone's concentration be so intense and yet not at all?

(And why is she always looking at what is invisible and not what shows
itself in good faith?)

You hate me, they say.

(The withholding demeanor of the one who feels truly alone will always be mistaken for scorn.)

(Because they can't read you, they assume the worst.)

(Because there is silence.)

(This is my silence, which is not silence at all, but bracketed speech.)

(If I close my eyes it's because I'm tired and not because I'm bored.)

And then when I feel myself falling I remember my dream in the flash of a sunflower opening behind my back. A tree losing itself to winter. There's nothing there by the time I turn around and everywhere I go my back is turned to the dream, until the moment I hear the latch open and the square of concrete beneath my feet dislodges. Where am I? Only Autochthons of The Book ask such questions. It is the mystery of a return without place. Excess of language without the anchor of land. All I can say of the desert is that it prepared me to receive The Book by showing me solitude: The Book of Questions.

"I miss you," I wrote in my journal. "I miss knowing myself so well it drives me crazy." In these pages: dreams of being shown the grace of work and not just desultory efforts or the inverted grace of falling apart. To know more than the way love inside the cave splits the skin on the knuckles.

Or the way the cave becomes a terrordome becomes the city that gave birth to neoliberal trade policies: the surveillance state *par excellence.*

(You are afraid. I could have told you that.)

LIKE THE BANKS
I MERGE TO BECOME
SOMETHING GREATER
THAN MYSELF

YOU MAKE THE IMPOSSIBLE MOUNTAIN JUST TO WEEP AT ITS FEET

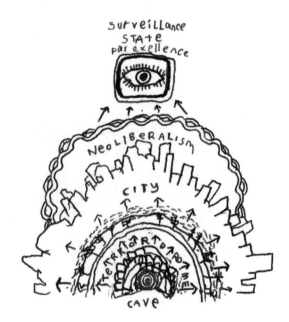

THE VERNACULAR OF OUR BODIES

What is this rattling
I sent for someone to come get me but where are they
where have they gone
where am I supposed to go if I am not got?
The woman sat sad
next to me on the plane.
She watched me. She looked at me again and again, gave me gum while
I was staring out the window. She followed me through the airport.
I didn't want to make her feel bad so I looked at her and smiled. She
wanted to know what I was and spoke to me in Spanish.

When outside I remember
I was crossing the street
the street crossed me, I became tar
I realized, I have been following her into the dream and I am lost.
She lost me.
I'm on the streets waiting for the giant hole to open.

Dear ----
I am living in your ghost and we are living in the bodies of our memories.

Your body next to my body is being rewritten. I hope that's okay. I dream of you every night and I worry that the more I dream the more I overwrite you, the more I re-write the memory of you. In the dream I am always struggling to explain something to you in the language we created, in Jumyung-hua. I'm gathering the lingual filaments to finally say what I came here to say. I speak to you in a strange blend of Chinese, English, and bodyspeak. And telepathy and intuition and the cosmic synchronization of unspoken understanding. In the dreams I am trying to say something and then—ah!—the revelatory moment. *Dong le, dong le!* Like when I explained I was queer and your eyes got wide and you got out your notebook and said, *Today is a good day.* But not in English.

You and the memories of you are ghosts. I want to write you without writing over you. I have something to tell you. That's what it's like in the dream. *Come here!* I have something to tell you. One night it was something rather meaningless. The urgent message was: "That woman is going to Japan." That woman . . . nage nuren yao qu riben. Sometimes I am confessing my love, or just trying to be witty around you so you'll like me.

You came into the sitting room when I was shaking and crying because I took two shots of soju and felt very alone. And when you came, I thought, This is what I wanted. You started crying too. A Canadian girl was like—*No! Not you too!* You told me about my future. I was allergic and fainted in the bathroom.

I try to map the dreams
but the bad ones surface like dead fish.
I'm writing into you.
I see your face.
You speak to me in the body vernacular.

I felt so fucking sick I had another bad dream this one was about her she
was on the same bus as me and then she got off and I followed her and
tried to explain that I didn't have anything planned and could I please
follow you, wo meiyou dasuan. And then the bus driver made fun of
my pronunciation and I repeated it slower. I was waiting for you to say,
lai ba. Come here.

I guess it's true that in most of the dreams you are afraid (of me?). Or
I'm afraid. I can't tell. I'm waiting for you and I know you're thinking,
Fuck off. But still I persist with our language, and on some nights you
understand. You turn to face me. You are with me inside it.

NATURA NON FACIT SALTUS

Having become embroiled in the strange
dream of the tree projected into emptiness
we had to see it through to its light.

I wrote to you about Simone Weil
the days spent circling the ruins of the
manor house, curled up and swaying

to recount the disease, a cloud of
airborne beetles erasing the grove
Trees succumb to the scourge of

summer and disappear, felled with
an infallible accuracy. The pressure
of night passes over the land. At

that very moment I register that
this doorway is without door, that
building had been made shell

by the unrelenting gusts of wind
bending this world out of shape.
I saw, I must have seen, it seemed

a terrible flickering, the wizened
world at the center of a black mass
of trees, shivering into dust. A

sediment of extinction is deposited
as a picture of an empty horizon. I
told you, did you believe me when

I said that everything down there
had been destroyed, then half-
reconciled at the threshold when

passing through the doorway I saw
the opening of the tree. What
calamity was redeemed by this

tree of coral, covered in gossamer
threads? At the center of the
unmade world is a tree that draws

its light
from the soil of everything
from the soil of everything negated.

[A MOMENT BREAKING LOOSE FROM THE PAST BECOMES THE VOICE INSIDE YOUR HEAD]

Where
in this architecture of dust
will you find the space to build
a house that does not split?

There

I see your hand
trying to escape
the raw activity
of laying stones

Formations
will spryly emerge
the dampened loam shaped
into something terrible

From the mud she tells me,
"Some days I wake up laughing because these forms are so unnecessary"
"Some days I wake up crying because these forms are so unnecessary"

But if you will have it
the hollow egg will fall
shrouded in
iridescent fish scales

This
is the texture of the 21st century
in the shadow cast by zero:
a fracture beneath the canopy
We wait for the rain to stop
and the answer to come in the
form of a simple question

But what good is a question
when a question flung in saltwater
drowns in saline night terrors?

"Go on, I'm listening"
No,
you're so goddamn busy
dreaming the particulate dream
of broken boughs
scattered across the dead zone
where the sound fails to circulate
and the question dies
in the silence of inert space

Here
there is no Friend
just the soundless reverberations of
the disappeared, an errant herd
of revenants who roam the
page in search of a body faithful
enough to hold the memory

Do you remember
the threads cast in your sleep
when you gently parted the soil
and planted the gift of her face?

These threads—which you secrete
when you believe no one is looking
allow me to trace the face you
make when I ask how a body
bathed in the blood of the nidus flood
sheds the nothing from which it springs

[You are free to void me.
That is what's at stake when I speak to you like this:
the one who is addressed is captured by the question
while the one who asks is diminished—is *humiliated*—
by the addressee's silence.]

We shall never know what the sunflower itself is.

D. H. LAWRENCE

She asked for nothing but her sex made its demands,
like a sunflower born in a tomb.

CLARICE LISPECTOR

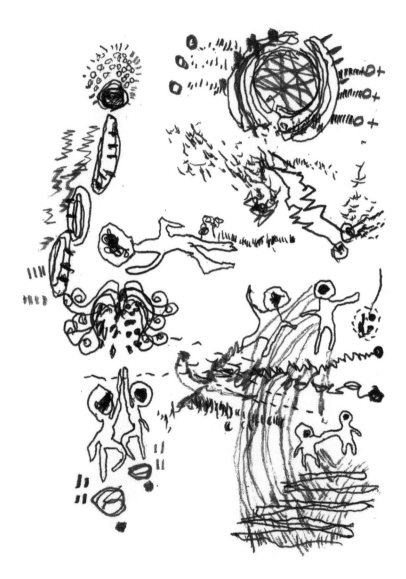

THE SUNFLOWER CAST A SPELL
TO SAVE US FROM THE VOID

Some

sunflowers

save their

daughters with invading

dreams distilled into layers of

singing ray petals that meet the eyes as

lemons, I don't remember, now the sunflower is an equation, now a
t-shirt,

> now lance or condition of heart, its Fibonacci radiance excreting
> phyllotactic spirals to light (in the absence of sun) *tomb*

*What is it about the sunflower, which appears in dreams to announce
every obsession? X of E=mc²? X of the infinity flower, its deep mathe-
matical order. I recruited K to help me solve the sunflower conjecture. M
wanted to help, but it was not his help I needed. Why did I want to be
seen by K while wearing the t-shirt of the sunflower equation? Emailed K*

about the problem, but did not respond after his initial response. Then I was walking into a building and he and E were huddled together looking at something on a computer. I was only wearing the sunflower t-shirt and black brief undies, so I left to plan my follow-up email. How would I hook him? Questions about technical details. Wanted to capture the whole of mathematics in my questions, to offset the mortification of being caught in my underwear. Outside the equation the whole city was turned into a saturnalia of commerce, everything was for sale. I watched a woman try on a button-down cowboy shirt and fur coat. Wanted to snatch the shirt off her body, believing it would make me lovable.

Fourth

sister

of inflorescence

in the room

where the caught breath is

shed between word I hear the annunciation roar

scattering yellow across the day and splintering the head with its blinding symmetry

A new iteration of the dream: "You were never no locomotive, Sunflower, you were a sunflower!" You were never yourself. You were octopus, you were the face of a book we won at the arcade. You were sutra, or a social movement in Taiwan.

You were primordial poultice. You were the composite self, until my coconspirator and I set out to turn you into ice cream. En route we passed a village of witches, outran the melting wedding cake. Who was the bride in the yellow dress from gagatown? The keeper of geological time. People on the train complained about the slowness of the Chinese Internet.

I

I don't

I don't remember

I don't remember anything, wait

I remember waiting, flinging seeds into a faux-

terracotta trough, then transferring my seedlings to the plant bed outside
the window

and waiting for the green spire to beget young Helios—a child who
lives to witness the miracle of anything that grows

ACKNOWLEDGMENTS

It takes a village to birth a book. Any attempt at giving thanks will surely be incomplete, but here goes . . .

First, I would like to thank my editorial team at Nightboat Books: Andrea Abi-Karam, Lindsey Boldt, and Stephen Motika. mg dufresne was the first person to provide editorial feedback on this manuscript and deserves a special thanks. Jorie Graham discovered the book's hidden inner structure by laying the pages of this manuscript out on her floor to rework the order. I would like to thank all the people I workshopped these poems with: Richard Greenfield, Connie Voisine, Jorie Graham, and everyone in Jorie's workshops, particularly Sherah Bloor, who went through the entire manuscript with me page-by-page. Thanks to Cassandra Troyan for publishing several of these poems in *The Fanzine* and for being a good comrade. Special thanks to Kalan Sherrard for doing the illustrations and to my dear friend Kit Schluter for designing the book.

A tender thanks to: Alexander Moll, Lily Hoang, LaKeyma Pennyamon, John DeWitt, Jack Frost, Nat Raha, Fred Moten, Amy Zanoni, Brandon Shimoda, Rona Lorimer, Sylvia Schedelbauer, Christopher Soto, Eric Linsker, Lara Lorenzo, Matthew Polzin, Emilie Connolly, Francesca Manning, Christina Davis, and everyone involved with Home School and Kundiman. Last but not least, I am endlessly grateful for my family: Danny, Randy, mom, and dad—thank you for your support.

JACKIE WANG is a poet, library rat, trauma monster, harpist, and Assistant Professor of Culture and Media Studies at The New School. She is the author of *Carceral Capitalism*, as well as the chapbooks *Tiny Spelunker of the Oneiro-Womb* and *The Twitter Hive Mind Is Dreaming*. When not writing poetry she researches race, surveillance technology, and the political economy of prisons and police.

NIGHTBOAT BOOKS

NIGHTBOAT BOOKS, a nonprofit organization, seeks to develop audiences for writers whose work resists convention and transcends boundaries. We publish books rich with poignancy, intelligence, and risk. Please visit nightboat.org to learn about our titles and how you can support our future publications.

The following individuals have supported the publication of this book. We thank them for their generosity and commitment to the mission of Nightboat Books:

Kazim Ali
Anonymous (4)
Jean C. Ballantyne
The Robert C. Brooks Revocable Trust
Amanda Greenberger
Rachel Lithgow
Anne Marie Macari
Elizabeth Madans
Elizabeth Motika
Thomas Shardlow
Benjamin Taylor
Jerrie Whitfield & Richard Motika

In addition, this book has been made possible, in part, by grants from the National Endowment for the Arts, the New York City Department of Cultural Affairs in partnership with the City Council, and the New York State Council on the Arts Literature Program.

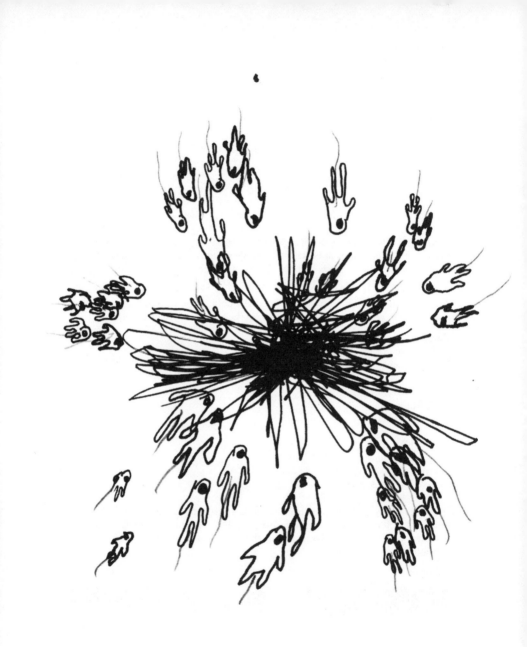